My Amazing Toddler Behavioral Series

I Have A BIG Job.
I Am A BIG SISTER!

An Affirmation-Themed Toddler Book
About Getting A Sibling (Ages 2-4)

By

Suzanne T. Christian

TWO RAVENS
BOOKS

Two Little Ravens
CHILDREN'S NON-FICTION BOOKS

Paperback Edition: 9781964202624
Hardcover Edition: 9781964202631
Digital Edition: 9781964202648

Published in the United States by Two Ravens Books LLC,
254 Chapman Rd, Ste 209, Newark DE 19702

'Expand the mind, free the imagination, one title at a time.'
www.tworavensbooks.com

An Affirmation Book for Toddlers
Becoming Big Sisters

This gentle and uplifting book is filled with simple, age-appropriate affirmations explicitly designed for toddlers adjusting to having a new sibling. As you read together, your child will discover what it means to be a caring and confident big sister while feeling reassured that they are still cherished.

Every page features sweet, relatable moments and colorful illustrations that reflect the joys and challenges of this significant change. Your toddler will embrace their new role with pride and compassion through positive repetition.

Make this book a cozy part of your reading routine, and enjoy watching your little one grow into their important job–with love, laughter, and lots of cuddles along the way!

Suzanne T. Christian

I am a big sister,
and this is my special job!

I share my favorite teddy
with Baby _____.

Gentle hands keep Baby _____ safe. I am a big sister!

I share my drawings so Baby _____ can see all the pretty colors.

I do a funny dance to make Baby _____ giggle.

My silly face makes Baby _____ laugh.

Baby _____'s
tiny toes make me smile.

If I feel sad, I ask Mommy for a hug.

I love to share my bedtime stories.
I am a big sister!

I wave hello when Baby _____ wakes up.

Baby _____ laughs when I blow raspberries.

pfft!

My family loves me and
Baby _____ so much!

If Baby _____
drops a toy,
I pick it up gently.

Mommy says I am
a good helper.
I am a big sister!

I wait patiently when Mommy feeds the Baby.

It's okay if
Baby _____
cries sometimes.
That's how babies talk!

My words are kind;
I am a big sister!

I help
Baby _____
learn new things
every day.

My soft voice helps Baby _____ sleep.
I am a big sister!

I help pick out tiny clothes
   for Baby_____.

My job is very important.
I am a big sister!

I Have A Big Job.
I Am A Big
SISTER!
The End!

My Amazing Toddler Behavioral Series

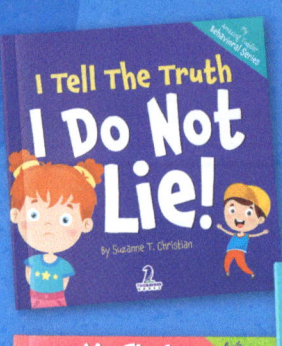

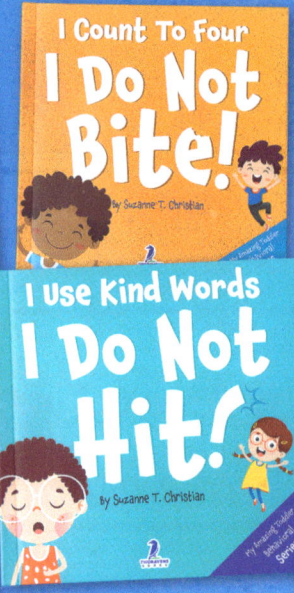

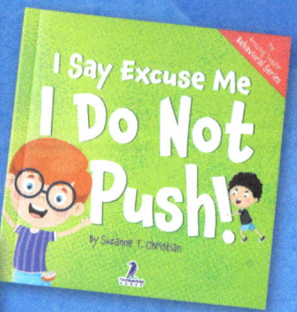

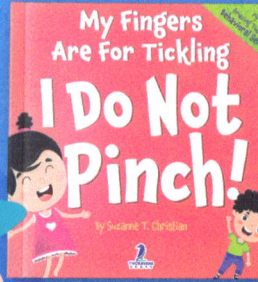

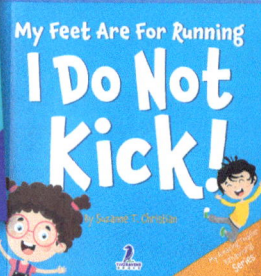

Check Out
Suzanne T. Christian's beloved series
'My Amazing Toddler Behavioral Series'.
Young readers are sure to enjoy!

Two Little Ravens
CHILDREN'S NON-FICTION BOOKS

Dear Amazing Reader,

Thank you for diving into **I Have A Big Job. I Am A Big Sister!** with me. If this book touched your heart or made a difference for a young reader, I'd be grateful if you could share your thoughts in a review. Your feedback inspires my future work and helps others discover the magic within these pages.

I'd love to hear from you directly if you have suggestions or ideas for improving the book. Please feel free to reach out to me at **suzanne.christian@tworavensbooks.com.** Your voice counts, and I cherish it deeply.

With heartfelt gratitude,